Motherhood

For Judy Hurrell, my Mum

First published in Great Britain in 1996 by Brockhampton Press,
a member of the Hodder Headline Group, 20 Bloomsbury Street, London WC1B 3QA.

This series of little gift books was made by Frances Banfield, Kate Brown, Laurel Clark,
Penny Clarke, Clive Collins, Melanie Cumming, Nick Diggory, Deborah Gill, David Goodman,
Douglas Hall, Maureen Hill, Nick Hutchison, John Hybert, Kate Hybert, Douglas Ingram,
Simon London, Patrick McCreeth, Morse Modaberi, Tara Neill, Anne Newman, Grant Oliver,
Michelle Rogers, Nigel Soper, Karen Sullivan and Nick Wells.

ISBN 1 86019 469 9
A copy of the CIP data is available from the British Library upon request.

Produced for Brockhampton Press by Flame Tree Publishing,
a part of The Foundry Creative Media Company Limited,
The Long House, Antrobus Road, Chiswick W4 5HY

Printed and bound in Italy by L.E.G.O. Spa.

C E L E B R A T I O N

Motherhood

Selected by Karen Sullivan

Softly, in the dusk, a
woman is singing to me;
Taking me back down the
vista of years, till I see
A child sitting under the
piano, in the boom of the
tingling strings
And pressing the small,
poised feet of a mother
who smiles as she sings.

D.H. Lawrence, *Piano*

1

No man is really successful until his mother-in-law admits it.

English joke

In his mother's heart no baby ever grows up completely, and in some mysterious fashion a part of every man remains a child, peculiarly his mother's even though they are estranged. In that case there is sorrow for them both but whatever sense of hurt or injustice a man may harbour, he knows in the depth of his soul, that his mother is waiting always for his return.

Dame Enid Lyons

Sweet dreams form a shade,
O'er my lovely infant's head.
Sweet dreams of pleasant streams,
By happy silent moon beams

Sweet sleep with soft down.
Weave thy brows an infant crown.
Sweet sleep Angel milk,
Hover o'er my happy child.

Sweet smiles in the night,
Hover over my delight.
Sweet smiles Mother's smiles
All the livelong night beguiles.

William Blake, *A Cradle Song*

The First Day at School.

A mother has an innate ability for aggravating the wounds of her off-spring's pride. This is inevitable since the relationship between mother and child is a most unnatural one; other species have the good sense to banish their young at an early age.

John Rae, *The Custard Boys*

It was very pleasant to receive such uncritical love, because it left me free to bestow love; my kisses were met by small warm rubbery unrejecting cheeks and soft dovey mumblings of delight.

Margaret Drabble, *The Millstone*

I have no name
I am but two days old –
What shall I call thee?
I happy am
Joy is my name –
Sweet joy befall thee!

William Blake, *Infant Joy*

No rosebuds yet dawn impearled
Match, even in loveliest lands,
The sweetest flowers in all the world –
A baby's hands.

Algernon Charles Swinburne, *A Baby's Hands*

Monday's child is fair
    of face
Tuesday's child is full
    of grace
Wednesday's child is
    full of woe
Thursday's child has
    far to go
Friday's child is
    loving and giving
Saturday's child
    works hard for his
    living
But the child that is
    born on the
    Sabbath day
Is bonny and blithe
    and good and gay.

Traditional

I like my mother because she makes me feel happy.

Emma, 6

Love me – I love you,
Love me, my baby;
Sing it high, sing it low,
Sing it as may be.

Mother's arms under you;
Her eyes above you;
Sing it high, sing it low,
Love me – I love you.

Christina Rossetti

The mother-ear is so close to the heart that it can hear the faintest whisper of a child.

Kate Douglas Wiggin, *The Birds' Christmas Carol*

There was a place in childhood that I remember well,
And there a voice of sweetest tone, bright fairy tales did tell,
And gentle words, and fond embrace, were given with joy to me,
When I was in that happy place upon my mother's knee.

Samuel Lover

One good mother is worth a hundred schoolmasters.

Anonymous

Cooking and cleaning can wait till tomorrow
For babies grow up, we learn to our sorrow.
So blow away cobwebs
Dust go to sleep
I'm rocking my baby
And babies don't keep.

Anonymous

The hand that rocks the cradle
Is the hand that rules the world.

W.R. Wallace

A mother understands what a child does not say.

Jewish proverb

Buttercup Pictures

A BOOK OF
CIRCLING SCENES

All mothers are rich
    when they love
    their children.
There are no poor
    mothers, no ugly
    ones, no old ones.
Their love is always
    the most beautiful
    of the joys.
And when they seem
    most sad, it needs
    but a kiss which
    they
receive or give to turn
    all their tears into
    stars ...

Maurice Maeterlinck

A baby is something you carry inside you for nine months,
in your arms for three years,
and in your heart till the day you die.

M. Mason

Every man, for the sake of the great blessed Mother in Heaven, and for
the love of his own little mother on earth, should handle all
womankind gently, and hold them in all honour.

Alfred, Lord Tennyson

If evolution really works, how come mothers only have two hands?

Ed Dussault

Even when we are grown
Inside we're little still
Our mother we are missing
With her love our hearts are filled
For though children do grow older
And their lives become their own
They always miss their mothers
And the comfort of her home.

Kitty Browne

19

A mother is a woman with
a twenty-five hour day,
who can still find an hour
to play with her family.

Iris Peck

Mothers Darling.

'Who was your mother?'
'Never had none,' said the child, with another grin.
'Never had any mother? What do you mean? Where were you born?'
'Never was born,' persisted Topsy; 'never had no father, nor mother,
nor nothin'. I was raised by a speculator.'

Harriet Beecher Stowe, *Uncle Tom's Cabin*

It seems to me that my mother was the most splendid woman I ever
knew ... I have met a lot of people knocking around the world since,
but I have never met a more thoroughly refined woman than my
mother. If I have amounted to anything, it will be due to her.

Charlie Chaplin

All women become like their mothers. That is their tragedy. No man does. That's his.

Oscar Wilde, *The Importance of Being Earnest*

A man who has been the indisputable favourite of his mother keeps for life the feeling of a conqueror, that confidence of success that often induces real success.

Sigmund Freud

No vision of his mother's face
When she so fondly would set free
Her darling child from her embrace
To roam till eve at liberty.

Emily Brontë, *Lines*

Mother, I need you. Though a woman grown,
Mine own self's arbitrator, mine own law,
My need of you is deeper than I've known.

Gladys May Casely-Hayford (Aquah Laluah), *To My Mother*

Love is a special way of feeling ...
It is the safe way we feel when we sit on our mother's lap with her
arms around us tight and close.

Joan Walsh Anglund, *Love is a Special Way of Feeling*

Who ran to help me when I fell,
And would some pretty story tell,
Or kiss the place to make it well?
My mother.

Ann Taylor, *My Mother*

 24

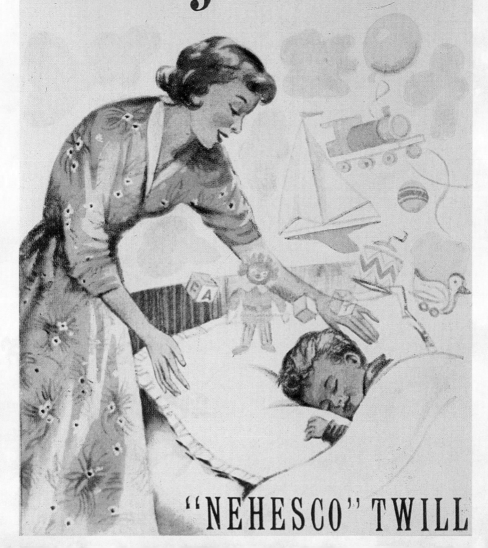

I was the light of my mother's life, and she was the light of mine.

Lauren Bacall, *Now*

Dear Mamma, if you just could be
A tiny little girl like me,
And I your mamma, you would see
How nice I'd be to you.
I'd always let you have your way;
I'd never frown at you and say,
'You are behaving ill today,
Such conduct will not do.'

Sydney Dayre (Mrs Cochran), *A Lesson for Mamma*

But there were pleasures in Mira's life: the
children themselves. They were a deep pleasure,
especially when she was alone with them and
wasn't anxious about preparing Norm's dinner,
or about their making noise. Holding their tiny
bodies, bathing them as they gurgled with
pleasure, oiling and powdering them while they
poked at her face or at their own, trying to figure
out what eyes and noses were, she would smile
endlessly, unconsciously. She had seen their
birth and the birth of her love for them as
miraculous, but it was just as miraculous when
they first smiled, first sat up, first babbled a
sound that resembled, of course, mama. The
tedious days were filled with miracles. When a
baby first looks at you; when it gets excited at

seeing a ray of light and like a dog pawing a gleam, tries to capture it in his hand; or when it laughs that deep, unselfconscious gurgle; or when it cries and you pick it up and it clings sobbing to you, saved from some terrible shadow moving across the room, or a loud clang in the street, or perhaps already a bad dream: then you are – happy is not the precise word – filled. Mira still felt as she had the first time she held Normie in the hospital, that the child and her feelings for it were somehow absolute, truer and more binding than any other experience life had to offer: she felt she lived at the blind true core of life.

Marilyn French, *The Women's Room*

My mother makes me fish fingers when I want them.

Ronak, 7

Womanliness means only motherhood
All love begins and ends there.

Robert Browning, *The Inn Album*

In today's fast-moving, transient, rootless society, where people meet
and make love and part without ever really touching, the relationship
every guy already has with his own mother is too valuable to ignore.

Ian Frazier, *Dating Your Mom*

Hundreds of stars in the
 pretty sky,
Hundreds of shells on
 the shore together,
Hundreds of birds that
 go singing by,
Hundreds of birds in the
 sunny weather.

Hundreds of dewdrops
 to greet the dawn,
Hundreds of bees in the
 purple clover,
Hundreds of butterflies
 on the lawn,
But only one mother the
 wide world over.

Anonymous, *Our Mother*

"*I never worry about the washing*"

RINSO
really *is* wonderful

THE Rinso way of washing is the way of science. The pure Rinso granules dissolve easily in water, and foam into a cleansing solution which works through the fibres of the cloth loosening the dirt without the necessity of rubbing. Rinsing then floats the dirt off and carries it away. There are no acids, no harsh chemicals in Rinso to harm clothes or hands. Rinso can be safely used cold or hot or boiling.

Rinso

The world's great labour saver

When you think of the life-and-death decisions
a mother makes every day – are they going to
have bicycles, can they go to the shops, can
they cross the road? – and she has only her
own judgement and knowledge to go by, and
the decision takes her about five seconds. Yet if
she worked in a vast company she wouldn't
dream of making such a recommendation
without memos and meetings and serious
deliberations, with experts and statistics to
back her up, and paid holidays to allow her to
recover from the strain of it all.

Fay Weldon

Today's your natal day;
    Sweet flowers I bring;
Mother accept I pray
    My offering.

And may you happy live,
    And long us bless;
Receiving as you give
    Great happiness.

Christina Rossetti

I'd walk a million miles
For one of your smiles
My mammie.

Al Jolson

This is an operation
demanding immense
determination, energy
and knowledge of how
to do the job most
efficiently. (By the job I
mean of course
motherhood.)

Elizabeth Longford

My mummy goes to work. She goes on aeroplanes
and talks. She drinks tea and has fun.

Bella, 7

James James
    Morrison Morrison
Weatherby George Dupree
    Took great
Care of his Mother
Though he was only three.

A.A. Milne, *Disobedience*

What is home without a mother?

Alice Hawthorne

So you are home! I'm so glad I could sing
That hills and streams with my singing would ring.
Home without you was a lamp without light
A flower without scent, a moonless night
I counted the days as they slowly slipped by
Like leaves off a tree, that are finished and die
Each withered brown leaf that dropped from the tree
Drew you steadfastly faithfully nearer to me.

Sarah Churchill, *For My Mother*

There is in all this cold
and hollow world no
fount of deep, strong,
deathless love, save that
within a mother's heart.

Felicia Hemans

An ounce of mother is
worth a pound of clergy.

Spanish proverb

Helping himself
to good health.......

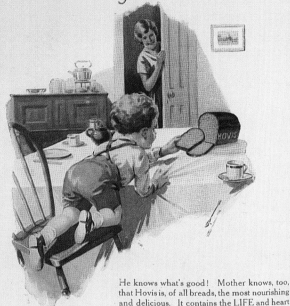

He knows what's good! Mother knows, too,
that Hovis is, of all breads, the most nourishing
and delicious. It contains the LIFE and heart
of the wheat. It builds bone and muscle.
No other bread is so rich in the health-giving
vitamins as well as in Phosphates which feed
brain and nerves. And so digestible, too!

TO HOUSEWIVES:
There is 25% of added
wheat-germ in HOVIS
a quarter of its entire
bulk. Let your next
loaf be HOVIS, but
for your own satisfac-
tion, be sure it *is*
HOVIS.

HōVIS

(Trade Mark)

Nourishing—and Nice

BEST BAKERS BAKE IT.

HOVIS LTD.   LONDON & MACCLESFIELD

Say, what is the spell, when her fledgelings are cheeping,
That lures the bird home to her nest?
Or wakes the tired mother, whose infant is weeping,
To cuddle and croon it to rest?
What's the magic that charms the glad babe in her arms,
Till it coos with the voice of the dove?
'Tis a secret, and so let us whisper it low –
And the name of the secret is LOVE!
For I think it is Love,
For I feel it is Love,
For I'm sure it is nothing but LOVE!

Lewis Carroll

She felt like the earth,
the mother of everything.

D.H. Lawrence, *The Rainbow*

On Mother's Day we got up first,
So full of plans we almost burst,
We started breakfast right away
As our surprise for Mother's Day.
We picked some flowers, then turned back
To make the coffee – rather black.
We wrapped our gift and wrote a card
And boiled the eggs – a little hard.
And then we sang a serenade,
Which burned the toast, I am afraid.
But Mother said, amidst our cheers,
'Oh what a big surprise my dears.
I've not had such a treat in years.'
And she was smiling to her ears!

Aileen Fisher

A little world he feels and sees;
His mother's arms, his mother's knees;
He hides his face against her breast,
And does not care to learn the rest.

Christopher Morley

My mother said, 'If just once more I hear you slam that old screen
door, I'll tear out my hair! I'll dive in the stove.' I gave it a bang and
in she dove.

X.J. Kennedy

I would desire for a friend the son who never resisted the tears
of his mother.

Lacretalle

A man loves his
sweetheart the most, his
wife the best, but his
mother the longest.

Irish proverb

My mother was the making of me. She was so true and so sure of me,
I felt that I had someone to live for – someone I must not disappoint.
The memory of my mother will always be a blessing to me.

Thomas Edison

She broke the bread into fragments and gave them to the children,
who ate with avidity.
'She hath kept none for herself,' grumbled the Sergeant.
'Because she is not hungry,' said a soldier.
'Because she is a mother,' said the Sergeant.

Victor Hugo

All that I am or hope to be, I owe to my angel mother.

Abraham Lincoln

She works at tasks
Requiring no especial skill,
Yet making their demons,
Hard to fulfil,
Demands on time and patience
And the capricious will.

Grease blears the gaze
Of water cooling in the bowl
And films her wrists and hands;
Toil takes its toll
Of strength, drains light and music
From the air and numbs the soul;

Or surely would
Except her love re-makes all things,
And every trivial chore,
Transmuted, brings
A sacramental joy
And, while she works, she sings.

Vernon Scannell

Sonnets are full of love, and this my tome
Has many sonnets: so here now shall be
One sonnet more, a loving sonnet from me
To her whose heart is my heart's quiet home,
To my first Love, my Mother on whose knee
I learnt love-lore that is not troublesome:
Whose service is my special dignity
And she is my lodestar while I go and come.
And so because you love, and because
I love you, Mother, I have woven a wreath
Of rhymes wherewith to crown your honoured name:
In you not fourscore years can dim the flame
Of love, whose blessed glow transcends the laws
Of time and change and mortal life and death.

Christina Rossetti

Be kind to your mother-in-law. Babysitters are expensive!

English joke

There is only one pretty child in the world, and every mother has it.

Proverb

What mother sings to the cradle goes all the way to the coffin.

Henry Beecher Ward

A child may have too much of his mother's blessing.

Scottish proverb

The law of heredity is that all undesirable traits come from the other parent.

Anonymous

The joys of parents are secret and so are their griefs and fears.

Francis Bacon, *Essays: Of Parents and Children*

Children suck the mother when they are young, and the father when they are grown.

English proverb

A spoilt child never loves its mother.

Sir Henry Taylor, *Notes from Life*

A Posy for Mother.

"A POSY for
　　　Mother,
　　because
　she's kind,
　The sweetest
　　flowers that
　　　I could
　　　find!"

"What do you
　　want for them?"
　　　　Mother said,
Tenderly patting
　　　the curly head.

"Twenty kisses,"
　　said Baby May—
"Dreadful ex-
　　pensive flowers
　　　　are they!"

But Mother
　bought them,
　　because, you know,
They meant:
　"Dear Mother,
　　I love you so!"

C. B.

If I were hanged on the highest hill,
Mother o' mine, O mother o' mine!
I know whose love would follow me still,
Mother o' mine, O mother o' mine!
If I were drowned in the deepest sea,
Mother o' mine, O mother o' mine!
I know whose tears would come down to me,
Mother o' mine, O mother o' mine!
If I were damned by body and soul,
I know whose prayers would make me whole,
Mother o' mine, O mother o' mine!

Rudyard Kipling, *Mother O' Mine*

There is no finer investment for any community than putting milk
into babies.

Sir Winston Churchill

GRAND SUMMER NUMBER ~ PACKED WITH HOLIDAY FEATURES

MOTHER

THE HOME MAGAZINE

6^{D.}

JULY 1939

A PARTY *at the* PALACE
INTIMATE STUDY OF
THE QUEEN AS HOSTESS

*THREE Complete Stories
and Romantic Serial*

BABYCRAFT ~ KNITTING ~ BEAUTY ~ FASHION

Know you what it is to be a child? ... It is to believe in love, to believe in loveliness, to believe in belief; it is to be so little that the elves can reach to whisper in your ear; it is to turn pumpkins into coaches, and mice into horses, lownesses into loftiness, and nothing into everything, for each child has its fairy godmother in its own soul.

Francis Thompson

They now have a mother-in-law sandwich: cold shoulder with salty tongue.

English joke

Blessed be childhood, which brings down something of heaven into the midst of our rough earthliness.

Henri Frederic Amiel

There will be a singing in your heart,
There will be a rapture in your eyes;
You will be a woman set apart,
You will be so wonderful and wise.
You will sleep, and when from dreams you start
As of one that wakes in Paradise
There will be a singing in your heart,
There will be a rapture in your eyes.

There will be a moaning in your heart,
There will be an anguish in your eyes,
You will see your dearest ones depart,
You will hear their quivering goodbyes.
Yours will be the heartache and the smart,
Tears that scald and lonely sacrifice;
There will be a moaning in your heart,
There will be an anguish in your eyes.

There will come a glory in your eyes,
There will come a peace within your heart;
Sitting 'neath the quiet evening skies,
Time will dry the tear and dull the smart.
You will know that you have played your part;
Yours shall be the love that never dies:
You, with Heaven's peace within your heart,
You with God's own glory in your eyes.

Robert Service, *The Mother*

Children are the anchors that hold a mother to life.

Sophocles

A rather diminutive army officer attended the regimental dance. Arriving late, he saw that everyone was dancing with the exception of one woman. Going up to her and bowing, he said: 'May I have the pleasure of this dance?'

Looking him up and down she replied somewhat haughtily, 'I don't dance with a child.'

Quick as a flash, he retorted, 'I am sorry, madam, I was not aware of your condition.'

Army joke

Mother knows best.

Edna Ferber

HER FAVOURITE

GROWING children need HOVIS. It provides essential nourishment which enables little bodies to keep pace with the rapid growth accorded by nature. HOVIS is richer in brain and body-building elements because it contains added wheat-germ. HOVIS is different from ordinary flour in that it has the richest part of the wheat *put back* into it.

HOVIS

(Trade Mark.)

Your Baker Bakes it

HOVIS LTD., MACCLESFIELD

Lady Macbeth: What beast was 't, then,
That made you break this enterprise to me?
When you durst do it, then you were a man;
And, to be more than what you were, you would
Be so much more the man. ... I have given suck, and know
How tender 't is to love the babe that milks me:
I would, while it was smiling in my face,
Have pluck'd my nipple from his boneless gums,
And dash'd the brains out, had I so sworn as you
Have done to this. ...

Macbeth: Bring forth men-children only!
For thy undaunted mettle should compose
Nothing but males.

William Shakespeare, *Macbeth*

When the voices of children are heard on the green
And laughing is heard on the hill,
My heart is at rest within my breast
And everything else is still.

William Blake, *Nurse's Song*

The precursor of the mirror is the mother's face.

D.W. Winnicott

She took after her mother who took after her father who took after
the maid.

English joke

Your last big morale-building letter was most appreciated. You are the most wonderful mummy that a girl ever had, and I only hope I can continue to lay more laurels at your feet. Warren and I both love you and admire you more than anybody in the world for all you have done for us all our lives. For it is you who has given us the heredity and the incentive to be mentally ambitious. Thank you a million times!
Your very own Sivvy

Sylvia Plath, *Letters Home*

For a mother the son always shines.

Proverb

Before becoming a mother I had a hundred theories on how to bring up children. Now I have seven children and only one theory: love them, especially when they least deserve to be loved.

Kate Samperi

Thou art thy mother's glass, and she in thee
Calls back the lovely April of her prime.

William Shakespeare, *Sonnets*

"Let it snow, we've got Daddy's Player's"

I was still unable to read but I was snobbish
enough to insist on having my books. My
grandfather went along to his scoundrel of a
publisher and was given *Les Contes* by Maurice
Bouchor, the poet, tales drawn from folklore
and adapted to children's tastes by a man, who,
so they said, still had the eyes of a child. I
wanted to begin my appropriation ceremonies
on the spot. I took the two small volumes,
sniffed at them, felt them, opened them
casually 'at the right page' and made them
creak. It was no good: I did not feel that I
owned them. I tried without greater success to
treat them as dolls, cradle them, kiss them and
beat them. On the verge of tears, I finally laid
them on my mother's lap. She looked up from
her work: 'What do you want me to read,
darling? About the Fairies?' I asked

incredulously: 'Are there Fairies in there?' I knew the tale well: my mother often told it to me while washing my face, breaking off to massage me with eau-de-Cologne, or to pick up, from under the bath, the soap which had slipped from her hands, and I would listen with half an ear to an all-too-familiar story ... all the while she was talking, we were alone and private, far from man, gods and priest, two does in the wood, with those other does, the Fairies; I never could believe that whole book could have been written to feature this episode in our profane life, which smelt of soap and eau-de-Cologne.

Jean-Paul Sartre, *Words*

Of all the rights of women, the greatest is to be a mother.

Lin Yutang

Children are a bridge to heaven.

Anonymous

A mother's warm encouragement,
The special help she lends,
Are the things that make her
What she is –
The very best of friends.

Anonymous

Your children are not
your children. They are
the sons and daughters
of life's longing for
itself ... you may strive
to be like them, but
seek not to make them
like you.

Kalil Gibran, *The Prophet*

In the eyes of its mother, every beetle is a gazelle.

Moroccan proverb

Looking at his Mammy
With eyes so shiny blue,
Makes you think that heaven
Is coming close to you.

Frank. L. Stanton

God could not be everywhere and therefore he made mothers.

Hebrew proverb

Notes on Illustrations

Page viii-1 *The Artist's Wife and Her Two Daughters*, by H. Marriot Paget (Christopher Wood Gallery, London). Courtesy of The Bridgeman Art Library; **Page 3** *A Morning Stroll*, by Dorothea Sharp (Whitford & Hughes, London). Courtesy of The Bridgeman Art Library; **Page 5** *The First Day at School*. Courtesy of The Laurel Clark Collection; **Page 6** *Sunlight Soap for Rest and Leisure* (Lever Bros Ltd, Cheshire). Courtesy of The Bridgeman Art Library; **Page 9** *Bob Apple*, by Frederick Morgan (Rafael Valls Gallery, London). Courtesy of The Bridgeman Art Library; **Page 10-11** *E to G from an Alphabet based on Old Nursery Rhymes*, by Walter Crane (Anthony Crane Collection). Courtesy of The Bridgeman Art Library; **Page 15** *Butter Cup Pictures*. Courtesy of The Laurel Clark Collection; **Page 16-17** *Going Home, 1873*, by Henry Woods (Warrington Museum & Art Gallery, Cheshire). Courtesy of The Bridgeman Art Library; **Page 19** *Mother & Child*, by William-Adolphe Bouguereau (Private Collection). Courtesy of The Bridgeman Art Library; **Page 20** *Mother Darling*. Courtesy of The Laurel Clark Collection. **Page 23** *Bed Time*, by A. Foord Hughes (Haworth Art Gallery, Accrington, Lancashire). Courtesy of The Bridgeman Art Library; **Page 25** *Sunny Dreams, Advertising Card for Nehesco Twill, 20th Century* (Private Collection). Courtesy of The Bridgeman Art Library; **Page 26** *Snowballs*. Courtesy of The Laurel Clark Collection. **Page 31** *Baby Picking Michaelmas Daisies*, by Dorothea Sharp (John Davies Fine Paintings, Stow-on-the-Wold, Gloucestershire). Courtesy of The Bridgeman Art Library; **Page 32-3** *First Steps, by* Joseph Israels (Bonhams, London). Courtesy of The Bridgeman Art Library; **Page 34** *I Never Worry about Washing – Rinso is Really Wonderful*. Courtesy of The Laurel Clark Collection; **Page 37** *More Haste Less Speed*, by Arthur John Elsley. (Fine Art of Oakham Ltd, Leicestershire). Courtesy of The Bridgeman Art Library; **Page 38-9** *The Child*, by Tom Mostyn (Charles Young Fine Paintings, London). Courtesy of The Bridgeman Art Library; **Page 40** *Pontus, 1890*, by Carl Larrson (National Museum, Stockholm). Courtesy of The Bridgeman Art Library; **Page 43** Helping Himself to Good Health . . . Hovis. Courtesy of The Laurel Clark Collection; **Page 45** *Mother and Daughter*, by Thomas Benjamin Kennington (Gavin Graham Gallery, London). Courtesy of The Bridgeman Art Library; **Page 48-9** E to G from An Alphabet Based on Old Nursery Rhymes, by Walter Crane (Anthony Crane Collection). Courtesy of The Bridgeman Art Library; **Page 51** *Mother and Child*, by Mary Gow (Victoria & Albert Museum, London). Courtesy of The Bridgeman Art Library; **Page 53** *Pears – Matchless for the Complexion*. Courtesy of The Laurel Clark Collection; **Page 54** *The Newborn Child*, by Theodore Gerard (Private Collection). Courtesy of The Bridgeman Art Library; **Page 57** *Mother and Children*, by Hippolyte Delaroche (Wallace Collection, London). Courtesy of

The Bridgeman Art Library; **Page 59** *A Posy for Mother*. Courtesy of The Laurel Clark Collection; **Page 61** *Fishing*, by Georgina de l'Aubiniere (Abbey Antiques, Hemel Hempstead, Hertfordshire). Courtesy of The Bridgeman Art Library; **Page 62** *Mother – The Home Magazine*. Courtesy of The Laurel Clark Collection; **Page 67** *Sunny Hours*, by Charles Lucy (Agnew & Sons, London). Courtesy of The Bridgeman Art Library; **Page 68** *Her Favourite, Hovis*. Courtesy of The Laurel Clark Collection; **Page 71** *Out of Reach, Daughters of Eve*, by Sir Frank Dicksee (Chris Beetles Ltd, London). Courtesy of The Bridgeman Art Library; **Page 72-3** *The Coming Nelson,* from the *Pears Annual, 1901*, by Frederick Morgan (A. & F. Pears Ltd, London). Courtesy of The Bridgeman Art Library; **Page 75** *Let it Snow, We've Got Daddy's Players*. Courtesy of The Laurel Clark Collection; **Page 79** *Preparing the Meal*, by William Lee Hankey (Whitford & Hughes, London). Courtesy of The Bridgeman Art Library; **Page 80-1** Advertisement for McVities, 1935. (*Illustrated London News*). Courtesy of The Bridgeman Art Library; **Page 83** *Good News*, by Isaac Snowman (Bonhams, London). Courtesy of The Bridgeman Art Library.

Acknowledgements: The Publishers wish to thank everyone who gave permission to reproduce the quotes in this book. Every effort has been made to contact the copyright holders, but in the event that an oversight has occurred, the publishers would be delighted to rectify any omissions in future editions of this book. Children's quotes printed courtesy of Herne Hill School; , 'For My Mother', Sarah Churchill, from *The Unwanted Statue,* reprinted courtesy of Leslie Frewan Publishers © Leslie Frewan Publishers; *The Women's Room*, Marilyn French, reprinted courtesy of Andre Deutsch; *When We Were Very Young*, A.A. Milne, reprinted courtesy of Methuen Children's Books and E.P. Dutton; *Disobedience*, A.A. Milne, reprinted courtesy of Methuen Children's Books and E.P. Dutton; *Words*, Jean-Paul Sartre, reprinted courtesy of Hamish Hamilton/Editions Galimard; *Letters Home*, Sylvia Plath, ed. Aurelia S. Plath, reprinted courtesy of Harper & Row; 'Mother O' Mine' by Rudyard Kipling, from *The Light that Failed*, reprinted courtesy of the National Trust; 'She Works at Tasks' Vernon Scannell, from *The Loving Game*, reprinted courtesy of Robson Books; 'The Mother', Robert Service, from *Rhymes of a Rolling Stone*, reprinted courtesy of Ernest, Benn, McGraw-Hill Ryerson Ltd, Toronto.